C000224652

in association with Pleasance
present

EPIC LOVE & POP SONGS

by Phoebe Eclair-Powell

Epic Love and Pop Songs received its world premiere on 6 August 2016
at Pleasance Dome, as part of the 2016 Edinburgh Festival Fringe

EPIC LOVE AND POP SONGS

by Phoebe Eclair-Powell

DOLL	Norah Lopez Holden
TED	George Caple
Director	Jamie Jackson
Designer	Anna Reid
Sound and Lighting Designer	Charley Mackley
Movement Director	Isla Jackson-Ritchie
Stage Manager	Andie Dew
Casting Director	Rebecca Targett
Producer	Callum Smith for Showroom

BIOGRAPHIES

Phoebe Eclair-Powell (Writer)
Phoebe is Channel 4 Playwright in residence at Soho Theatre. Credits include *TORCH* for Flipping the Bird (Latitude Festival/Underbelly Fringe); *Fury* (runner-up Verity Bargate Award, winner of Soho Young Writers' Award, nominated for Best New Play Offies 2016, Soho Theatre 2016); *WINK* (nominated for four Offies including Most Promising New Playwright 2015, Theatre503) and *Bangin' Wolves* for Courting Drama and Poleroid Theatre (Bush Upstairs/Wilderness Festival).

Phoebe was on the Royal Court Young Writers' programme 2013, the Soho Writer's Lab 2014, and Channel 4 Screenwriting course for 2015.

Jamie Jackson (Director)
Jamie's recent credits include *Tracy* (Underbelly); *Another Way* (Interval Productions); *Primadonna*, *SKINT* (VAULT Festival); *Muted* (Interval Productions); *The Pooki* (Tara Finney Productions/Park Theatre Script Accelerator programme); *WINK* (Theatre503); *The Natives* (Old Vic/Old Vic New Voices); *Alice Through the Looking Glass* (Iris). Associate director credits include *The Savage* (Live).

Anna Reid (Designer)
Anna is a set and costume designer based in London and is a graduate of Wimbledon College of Art.

Designer credits include *Fury*, *Brute* (Soho); *For Those Who Cry When They Hear the Foxes Scream* (Tristan Bates); *Tape* (The Drayton Arms); *Primadonna*, *SKINT* (VAULT Festival); *Dottir* (The Courtyard); *Dry Land* (Jermyn Street); *Bruises* (The Tabard); *Arthur's World* (Bush); *Hippolytos* (Victoria and Albert Museum); *Fierce* (Camden People's Theatre); *Hamlet* (Riverside Studios); *Macbeth* (ADC Theatre/various US venues). www.annareiddesign.com

Charley Mackley (Sound and Lighting Designer)
Charley has been a dance music producer since 2003 and is researching a PhD in sound design for theatre.

Recent theatre credits include *Clay*, *Girl From Nowhere* (Pleasance); *Brute*, *Sophie Wu is minging, she looks like she's dead*, *Lines in the Sand* (Soho); *Starlore for Beginners, and Other Plays* (Theatre503); *The View from Down Here* (Ovalhouse).

Isla Jackson-Ritchie (Movement Director)
Isla's movement direction credits include *Coal Eaters*, *WINK* (Theatre503); *Alice Through The Looking Glass* (St Paul's Church; *This Is Your Life* (Wilderness Festival); *Tell Me a Secret* (Airborne Theatre Edinburgh Fringe Festival); *Into The Dark* (Stage at Leeds); *SKINT* (VAULT Festival).

Callum Smith (Producer)
Callum is a theatre producer based in Glasgow. Previous productions include Scottish tours of *Blackout, How You Gonna Live Your Dash, Love 2.0* and *Couldn't Care Less* and Edinburgh Fringe productions including *Faslane, Denton and Me* (Made in Scotland 2016), *The Post Show* and *Bonny Boys are Few*. He has worked for some of the country's most prestigious theatres, including National Theatre of Scotland, Tron Theatre and the Royal Court, where he held the post of International Administrator.
www.callum-smith.co.uk

George Caple (TED)
George graduated from RADA in July 2016.

Theatre whilst training includes *Pains of Youth, Chez Feydeau, No One Sees the Video, All's Well That Ends Well, The Basset Table, Coriolanus, Electra, Philistines* and *The Accrington Pals*. Television includes *Doctors* (BBC).

Norah Lopez Holden (DOLL)
Norah graduated from RADA in July 2016.

Theatre whilst in training includes *Mr Puntilla and His Man Matti, Pains of Youth, In Arabia We'd All Be Kings, The Bright and Bold Design, The Winter's Tale, The Basset Table, Antony and Cleopatra* and *Electra*. Radio includes *A Charles Paris Mystery – The Cinderella Killer* for BBC Radio 4.

Showroom is a Glasgow-based theatre company committed to supporting the most exciting independent artists and small companies. Led by producer Callum Smith, the company aims to reduce the administrative burden placed upon artists who produce their own work by providing company structure and producing support to innovative new work. Recent projects include *Faslane* and *How You Gonna Live Your Dash* by Jenna Watt, *Denton and Me* by Sam Rowe Theatre and *Blackout* by Mark Jeary/New Room Theatre.

www.weareshowroom.co.uk | @WeAreShowroom | facebook.com/WeAreShowroom

Showroom would like to thank the following amazing people for donating to our FringeFunder campaign, and making the production possible:

Adam Morley, Aileen Sherry, Andrew McGregor, Alison Jackson, Ben Hargreaves, Conel Wingrave, Dan Ayling, Daniel Nixon, Deirdre O'Halloran, Ed Chalk, Elaine Bryceland, Eszter Marsalko, Eve Nicol, Genevieve Dawson, Geoffrey Powell, Jack P, Jane Boothroyd, Janet Ellis, Jenn Murray, Jenny Eclair, Kate Robbins, Maria Hannah, Marie-Claire Boyle, Michael Sparkes, Milly Thomas, Niall Wilson, Patrick Holt, Peter Genower, Rhona McCallum, Sara Hargreaves, Sarah Henley, Serafina Cusack, Sophia Satchell-Baeza, Sophie Neild, Suzann Smith, Tara Finney, Tristram Bawtree and Will Bourdillon.

And many thanks to the following people and organisations who helped us make the show:

Amy, Matthew and all the staff at the Pleasance; Vicky Featherstone and the Royal Court Theatre; Sean McGonigal; Old Vic New Voices; Schools Plus; West London Free School; Mac Cosmetics; Alison Jackson; Grace Sims, Mill Goble, Jack Hudson, Flipping the Bird Productions, and all the staff at the Edinburgh Festival Fringe society for their part in staging the best festival in the world.

EPIC LOVE AND POP SONGS

Phoebe Eclair-Powell

Acknowledgements

Thank you to Jamie Jackson, who is my Ted. Forever.

Thank you to my mum and dad for their constant support this year. And as ever – thank you, Mum, for being an incredibly fast reader.

Thank you, Mr Callum Smith, for making me take the risk – no regrets. Really – thank you.

Thank you, Amy Clamp and Matthew Dwyer and all at the Pleasance for taking a big punt – I am very, very grateful.

Thank you, Isla Jackson-Ritchie, because you are just a bit too awesome.

Thank you to my very first Doll and Ted – the excellent Norah Lopez Holden and George Caple.

Thank you to Anna Reid, Charley Mackley and Andie Dew – what a fantastic crew.

Thank you to my agent, the lovely Ikenna Obiekwe.

Thank you to the dude that is Dan Nixon – I owe you lots.

P.E-P.

Characters

DOLL, *sixteen, a liar (?)*
TED, *sixteen, a hero (?)*

Ted and Doll are the storytellers and this play is all about how you spin a tale. The set is negotiable, there could be a bed and a chair, a teenage bedroom from which a world is created, or nothing at all.

The title of this play mentions pop songs – use as many as you can/like to underscore the action – or they could even sing/perform certain songs. Keep it contemporary and relevant to you – though Beyoncé should probably stay the same – as I'm sure she won't be going out of fashion any time soon...

A forward slash (/) in the text indicates that the next person should interrupt the previous speech slightly. It is important to keep a rhythm and a pace with this play.

An ellipsis (...) means there is a slight moment of pause.

A dash (–) means the next person's line comes in straight away, not so much an interruption as a continuation.

This text went to press before the end of rehearsals and so may differ slightly from the play as performed.

DOLL. Hello, my name is Doll Evans and this is my show. And
it is a one-woman show with supporting material – a backing
dancer if you will – you know like one of them women that
sing in a black dress at the back of the stage on *Britain's Got
Talent* and wave their arms a bit – except my one's a man
and he's called Ted Parker. But forget about him, because
this is about me. And this is a list of things I like:

I like dunkin' biscuits in tea and then downing all the bitty
bits in the bottom of the cup. I like watching *Dinner Date* on
ITV3 because it reminds me that at least I'm not that much
of a freak. I like wearing these pyjamas every night even
though the towelling starts to smell of fanny really quickly,
you know how it all rides up, well it does.

I go to Harris Academy and I'm in Year 10 don't ya know,
yadda yadda I'm giving background, trust me it helps.

I'm really average is basically what I am trying to say,
I really, really am just that teenage girl you all know and
won't sit next to on the back of the bus. That one. Music too
loud brap brap I don't care, feet up on the seat, likes to link
arms, laughs at everything and thinks 'you're well fit' is the
best chat-up line ever. I'm her.

I live with my mum, cos well, that's the way it's always
been, but my dad lives round the corner, with Auntie Cheryl
who is both my aunt and my stepmum. Jezza Kyle ain't seen
nuthin yet. Get me a double-page spread in *Take a Break*.

But no really it's fine. As my mum would say 'no really
everyone I think you'll find IT'S FINE'. And then she chews
on some more HRT and puts a nicotine patch on her nipple.

I think I'm what's pushing Mum over the edge at the
moment to be honest.

Her blood pressure is well high and you can hear her teeth gnashing together in her sleep from my room. Except when she's like, crying.

I think it's because I'm pregnant.

Ta-dah.

I love a reveal don't you?

Trust me I'm not trying to be a bit-part in *Hollyoaks* it just sort of happened and then you think, 'well why not eh?' A little thing, round here, could be fun. I thought Mum would be more excited, she's always going on about me growing up and having nothing to live for blah blah, so now we both have something to live for – don't we?

I thought it was a great plan, but she was, well she was... I think it's cos I couldn't tell her who the father was. Sorry, but it's a secret – I might not even tell you guys.

TED. She won't even tell me.

DOLL. This is Ted – he's just here to make some things clear, and sometimes play other people, but that's all, cos it's my story, isn't it.

TED. Yeah course.

DOLL. And it's important that I tell it, isn't it?

TED. Yeah no / I

DOLL. Okay so this is a bad thing, but I thought being pregnant would sort of make people notice me at school, people like, you know, Samantha Hogan, because I'm not really that popular, not in the bottom lot, oh my god I'm not Chloe Wong who fingered herself during physics and was totally caught out – 'trying to pull her tights up' my arse, we all saw, bitch. Anyway I'm not friends with the shit lot, I'm not friends with a bunch of retard, four-eyes, spaccy-legs, dumb-tits, no-tits, fuckwits. No I'm like, um, well when they found out my stepmum was also my auntie the others just all sort of, well I wasn't at the top any more. Whevs.

Fine whatever, ignore me, I'll pull your hair harder and make you fucking scream, Samantha Hogan. Call me a psycho, bitch.

But for some reason being preggers just made it worse. Everyone's all awkward really actually basically, because they're all lying when they say they've had sex. And I wasn't, I wasn't lying at all. Proof.

I just didn't expect it to make me a social retard, oh wait do I mean reject. Basically um not that girl.

Then he starts being my friend. Don't you, Ted.

And then I'm not so alone any more.

TED. I become her mate because I don't have many, well any, not after what happened – and you're safer in a pair. And because I fancied her a bit, but I am a teenager and fancy most people, so you know. And because, well, because the way they treated her was cruel, and I knew what that felt like. I knew what it felt like to wake up sweating at the thought of being trapped with them, with people who seem to actually hate you in one classroom all day – figuring out ways to make yourself so small you turn / invisible

DOLL. No that's not, sorry don't listen to his bit, cos he has a way of spinning the shit side of things actually and I'm all about the positives. So sit down and wait for the bits when I tell you to speak like we agreed okay –

Okay?

TED *nods and sits*.

So he starts to be my friend, and at first I'm like oh really – this freak, because people sort of think Ted's a bit of a wet weirdo – sorry but they do, babe, but after a bit of time, I get used to it and then, well then we're inseparable.

And it makes life that little bit more bearable because Mum's being a nutter and a mutterer, and Dad doesn't want to know because it makes him feel sick, and Auntie Cheryl won't stop knitting baby booties in all the colours of the rainbow just in case it's a boy or a girl or an inbetweeny 'because they deserve booties too'. Apparently.

He makes it all make sense, even when everyone in the street is whispering and pointing, sniggering and laughing, I know why, it's because I'm a walking, talking cliché ain't I, really?

TED. But it's not that unusual is it. It's not that / odd

DOLL. No shut up.

Because you've already lied once tonight.

TED. Fine – the real reason I'm her friend, everyone, the real reason is because of her, because of Bethany, you / see

DOLL. Positives, positives, blue skies, and rainbows and reindeer and unicorns and blah blah blah blah blah.

My story, my story, mine.

Get over it.

Pause.

Sorry.

So anyway everything is bang tidy until one night we're watching *X Factor* as you do and suddenly my mum pounces like she just goes ape shit and starts screaming at him, 'YOU'RE THE DAD, YOU'RE THE DAD' effing and blinding, our dinner is all over the place, and she's sobbing now, and asking for her e-cigarette.

And we were just laughing because no, we've never, come on, Mum, this isn't the film *Juno*; he's a virgin for fuck's sake.

TED. All right.

DOLL. Sorry but you are, babe, and no, putting your limp dick in Pippa 'the chubster' Fulton does not count. And she was sick on you afters.

TED. It was only limp because JK made me do a spliff in the garden and it was definitely not weed but skunk and that's well stronger.

DOLL. Don't show off.

No one's interested in that.

No one cares about that actually.

Anyway I've done MDMA.

TED. No you haven't.

DOLL. I have.

TED. Whilst pregnant?

DOLL. Maybe.

TED. Exactly you haven't.

You'd have a kid with no teeth or three eyes or something horrid like that.

DOLL. Fine it was a really expensive smashed bit of paracetamol mixed with one of them Pro Pluses – and a tiny bit of speed.

Shit what if it has no ears or nose bits and I have to look after it extra specially.

Probs get loads more attention then.

So actually in a way…

And Katie Price copes with her first one, you know the big one –

TED. Harvey… I don't think you should really say stuff like that, / Doll

DOLL. Yeah so if she can do that I'll be fine.

In fact it would make it even more special.

I'd just be an extra-special super-mum.

Which I think I most definitely will be.

Won't I?

Won't I?

Ted, won't I?

TED. Yes, Doll – you're gunna be stellar.

DOLL. So anyway time passes – like it, well like it does and I'm now like pretty fucking pregnant – not like fat pregnant, but like it's pretty fucking obvious and I've had to buy extra-large school shirts from Evans like Amanda Davies has to – but she's got a 'hormone problem'. So anyway we go to school, me and Ted, and people have sort of just accepted that we come as a pair now, and we sort of get on with our lives and shit, except people start saying:

TED. 'Shouldn't you be having it by now?'

DOLL. and

TED. 'Where's a picture of it?'

DOLL. and

TED. 'Show us yer udders.'

...

Like they don't believe her.

DOLL. And then my mum starts saying:

TED. 'Right when's the next doctor appointment?'

DOLL. and

TED. 'We need to book this in'

DOLL. and

TED. 'Can I feel it kicking because at this stage?'

DOLL. Yadda yadda blah bluk whevs.

TED. Like she doesn't really believe her.

DOLL. Basicalemente people are getting on my tits about the lack of baby evidence – well fuck 'em yeah because I'm having it, it just doesn't happen like it does on TV yeah it takes time. Nine bleeding months, okay well no because I'm like six or seven months down the line, but still I got all the time. And yes I can come to your party, Samantha Hogan, even though you didn't invite me because no it will not harm my baby if I bump and grind and actually one vodka coke is actually allowed.

TED. You sort of had five though so...

DOLL. Everyone making out like I'm already a shit mum, like they all get to decide.

I won't be shit actually.

I'm going to be stellar.

TED. Of course you will, Doll – see we have an idea, in fact we have it all mapped out.

It's going to work really well – we came up with it that night.

Oh go on, Doll, don't do that face – I like this story.

DOLL. But it's not part of the –

TED. It makes us seem a bit nicer though I think.

DOLL. Oh for fuck's sake – Fine!

TED. That night at Samantha Hogan's party –

DOLL. Which we were not invited to –

TED. No we were not invited to.

We gatecrashed, because no one tells Doll what she can and can't do right she has this way of just – I dunno sticking two fingers up to pretty much everyone really.

And that felt... liberating.

DOLL. You are so sad sometimes it hurts.

TED. And we get in there – we get in that party and Samantha's parents have this tub thing right – they have a fucking hot tub in their garden and everyone is chilling in it, like people are topless for fuck's sake, just sitting topless in it and drinking which I think is a bit dangerous actually, and they're all shouting at Doll to get in –

DOLL. But I can't because I'm fucking pregnant and Ted – well let's just say that Ted isn't the world's most comfortable with his own –

TED. No, that's not – I get scared of the water, I have a thing about putting my head under the water –

It's a complex.

DOLL. Seriously why are you like this?

And this guy tries to push him in.

In fact all the guys are trying to push him in – and there's a gang of them right – and they're crowding round him – pushing him, swearing at him.

And I hear one say –

TED. What did they say, Doll?

DOLL. I hear them say… 'I wonder if this is how scared his / sister was'

TED. And that's when she did it – didn't you, Doll?

DOLL. I pissed in my big fake red plastic cup because Samantha Hogan thinks she's fucking cool – and has red plastic cups at her party like she's in *Mean Girls* or something. And I threw it in.

I threw it in and they all went mental.

TED. And we ran for it – we fucking legged it and my heart had never felt like that.

DOLL. We sat in a park till 2 a.m. on a seesaw – him up, me down, because well – look at him.

TED. And you told me that we were gunna look after this baby together – didn't you, Doll.

DOLL. Yeah I did, Ted.

TED. You said – we are gunna make this stellar.

DOLL....

    Yeah I did.

    ...

    But in the meantime to stop the umming and the ahhing, we need to find Mum something to distract her from the question-making and this finger-pointing and the dull, dull days of her sad little life – like Dad's moved on and so should she, just embarrassing otherwise and no one needs that.

    So we hatch a plan, me and Ted, because Ted's actually quite good at hatching plans.

TED. I was in Cubs.

DOLL. No wonder everyone thinks you're a bender.

TED. Doll, you said you wouldn't –

DOLL. Alright don't get your G-string in a twist – I'm not gunna tell them about what happened on the geography trip to Castlefield.

TED. *The plan* is to get Doll's mum a boyfriend, a nice one obviously –

DOLL. Well an alright one, because there ain't many blokes to chose from:

    We've got Denny down the pub –

TED. Fynn round the bike shop – too young –

DOLL. And Michael the postman who was fucking next-door Shannon's mum for ages but it all ended in a really great showdown involving smeared shit on toast.

TED. Denny is our number-one target

    We hack into her mum's Facebook.

DOLL. Not hard, she left it open.

TED. And we add him so that he knows she's interested.

DOLL. And a couple of other randoms just in case.

Mum's too thick to know that anyone's even tampered with it.

TED. Then we beg for a pub lunch that Sunday – a special treat before the baby's born.

DOLL. And my mum raises an eyebrow.

TED. 'If it ever is.'

DOLL. She says… if it ever is…

TED. What does she mean by that?

Doll?

Doll?

What did she mean by that?

Doll?

DOLL. So we hook my mum up with Denny who she always thought had a BO problem and grubby hands like he's dipped them in too many jars of pickled onions – but a couple of hints here and there that someone might actually like her and she's practically shoving her tits over the bar and ordering that:

TED. 'One more glass of dry white wine. Can't beat a bit of that to get the party started.'

DOLL. And Denny's not fussy.

TED. 'Ooh that is a large glass, titter titter titter.'

DOLL. Christ.

Denny and Mum have really loud sex, loud enough to make you want to puke into your own ears.

TED. But it's an alright price to pay for your mum's distraction –

DOLL. because suddenly there ain't no more questions, instead, even better, she starts taking evening shifts at the pub.

I have the whole house to myself.

TED. Result.

DOLL. I decide to have a party.

TED. A baby shower if you will.

DOLL. But with alcohol.

This will show everyone at school that this is happening for real. Except fuck off, Samantha Hogan, you are not coming round.

Tango in the fridge, and crisps in a big bowl that Mum bought for 'occasions' – as if anyone ever comes over – sad. I wait in the living room. I've even bought a banner that says – 'Congratulations, it's a Girl'. Because didn't I tell you, yeah it's a girl apparently. How fucking great is that?

I put Beyoncé on loud, yeah, yeah fuck it she's great, you all love her, she's all we need, DRUNK IN LOOOOVE. I drink five glasses of winergy – that's white wine and red bull – try it some time, does the job keeps you up, up, up.

I keep dancing in my living room, fuck it, I break the lamp by the telly by accident, except I didn't need to kick it twice maybe – it's the hormones.

Twat.

No one comes.

Why does nobody come, Ted?

TED. Okay so the truth is, I also become Doll's mate because, even though everyone else thinks she's a bit of a psycho – to be fair she did pull out a chunk out of Samantha Hogan's hair – though most of it wasn't hers to begin with anyway – I see something else, I see someone who needs looking after. And I suppose that's what I wanted – to find someone I could – I dunno – 'rescue' after what happened to my sister. It's sort of easy to figure that one out yeah – it's just 'displacement', that's what the psychologists call it.

And she looked like she really needed looking after. Scabby bruised legs, pale cheeks, wired and really tired at the same

time, stare you out with panda eyes, chewing her gum so
hard she would chip her teeth and flick the bits at you.
Coming into school with knee-high socks and this – bump –
this thing that no one could quite understand how she'd
managed to get inside her. Everyone was just a bit well,
scared of her.

...

I came, Doll. I came to your party.

DOLL. Fine. No one comes – Except Ted.

Surprise, surprise.

For once Ted lets his hair down and has a whole two cans of
lager and a shot of winergy.

TED. It was two shots of winergy actually.

Anyway – we dance to 'Drunk in Love'.

DOLL. He is not good at being Jay Z.

I'm fucking great at being Beyoncé.

TED. And we're dancing real close all of a sudden, like weirdly
close and we sort of start to –

DOLL. and I think it all just gets a bit –

and fucking hell this is –

but I think we might even –

TED. Maybe –

DOLL. start to –

TED. and it all feels like –

DOLL. and he's almost sort of in there…

And because at this point it's all a bit hard to deny it –

TED. That's when she tells me her big secret.

She's not pregnant.

At all.

You can buy fake bumps on the internet.

Pictures of other people's baby scans.

Take pills to stop your periods.

She hasn't even ever had sex, just given lots of um…

DOLL. You can say the word blowjob, Ted.

TED. Fine 'blowjobs', until now I suppose.

DOLL. Hold your horses it's not like you popped your cherry proper because I'm soon sicking up winergy all over the Freeview box and it's safe to say the party and the moment are both over.

Ted says I can blame the sick on him.

TED. Which she does.

After that her mum never offers me anything, not even a milky tea like usual.

But it's okay, because I'm hardly going round any more.

I'm a bit confused you see…

The truth is…

DOLL. Here he goes again –

TED. The truth is, I thought…

I thought you needed looking after, Doll, actually – and that the baby – the baby I thought you were having – could be a sort of –

Um, okay don't think me mental but – reincarnation.

Of her.

My sister.

You see the baby was due on the same day as her birthday.

You said it once in front of all our class.

May 19th.

DOLL. I so don't think I / did

TED. Yeah you did – May 19th.

Her birthday – my sister's birthday.

And I thought it was a sign and that my mum might even want to come back from abroad and help me look after it. Because no it wasn't mine, wasn't anyone's... but people thought it was.

Doll's mum wasn't the only one pointing, nodding.

They all thought it was mine.

DOLL. I don't see what this has got to do with my / story

TED. I thought it could belong to me as well.

A shared thing.

Small thing, to look after and keep safe.

DOLL. Boring.

TED. It could be the one thing to make my mum come home.

To make my mum think about someone new.

DOLL. Well don't cry about it.

TED. Not just her all the time.

DOLL. Oh for fuck's sake here we go.

TED. For once, this baby would make everyone see me.

And that's why she did it I suppose – Bethany, my sister.

To be / seen.

DOLL. Ted?

TED. Yes, Doll.

DOLL. Your sister.

TED. What about her?

DOLL. Got what she deserved.

Now sit down and shut up about your sad little povvo pot of family members.

Got it.

Great.

Good.

…

After I tell Ted about the whole, um not-actually-being-so-pregnant-after-all thing, Ted ignores me like some prick for ageees, like long, like a whole month and it gets pretty lonely when you're basically a billy what's-his-face no-mates.

I try talking to Chloe Wong but even she ain't having it.

And then one day in like Home Economics which everyone is ignoring because it is LONG –

TED. It was Maths actually –

DOLL. Which is still LONG…

Samantha Hogan rears her butt-ugly but some reason everyone thinks 'fit as fuck' face.

Go on, Ted – your time to shine.

I said GO ON.

TED, *still pissed off, becomes Samantha Hogan and delivers her lines.*

TED. 'We know the truth, fucktard.'

DOLL. 'What?'

TED. 'We know the truth.'

DOLL. And she looks me up and down – you have to look me up and down, Ted.

Yeah like that.

So she looks me up and down, do it again then, like she's thinking about setting me on fire. Like she's striking a really big long match up and down my body.

Till my hair is burning.

Burning fast like that woman –

What's-her-tits?

Ted?

Ted, who am I meaning?

Oh my god you can't do this bit and not answer me – Ted, who am I meaning? The one who thought she was having some sort of thing with God, like he was in her head?

TED *doesn't answer.*

Like a schizo.

Please, Ted, fuck's sake.

TED *doesn't answer.*

Joan of Arc that one.

See, I can do this without you, Ted – can't I?

Yeah like Joany just bubbling there.

With everyone watching us, and my skin, my skin is melting and I can't breathe because all the oxygen in my mouth is turning into smoke, like a dragon of oil and my neck is charring like coal fires on barbecues, and my eyes explode in their sockets because they can't stand the heat any more. I can't stand this heat. They stare at me and their eyes are sending more sparks of fire till I'm sizzling like a burnt sausage, my skin erupting from my sides.

'We know the truth' she says again and again, Ted...

TED. 'We know the truth.'

DOLL. And I think fuck it, he's told them, he has, hasn't he and what? – What's she gunna do like tell the whole school. I think – can I run? How fast can I run like right now?

TED. 'We know that no one turned up at your stupid baby shower.'

DOLL. And I can breathe, so much so that I smile as I call her a 'stupid cunt' and she smacks me in the nose and it's only bloody bleeding, 'you fucking hit a pregnant woman you psycho' – and they're laughing, the whole class is laughing at me – well take a fucking picture of it, you fuckwits, which they do actually – it goes round school like fucking norovirus all afternoon.

But worst of all, Ted is laughing with them. Right. Well then.

Even him.

Even you.

And I run to the bathroom not just for my nose but to check that it's all still there.

It's still there.

The padding, the bump.

It's still there.

But I'm feeling something wet run down my chin and as I sit on the floor it falls onto my shirt and my skirt and it's red and bold and blood.

And it sits on my school skirt like period, like I've leaked all over the place – which is just really annoying, and for a second it feels like maybe I'm losing it.

Like I'm losing it for real.

Because suddenly I can feel this life inside me that I will do everything to fight for and protect.

I'm not letting this go.

I'm not letting this stop.

I stick a load of tissue up my nose –

Not paying a few quid for a crusty old tampon.

Get toxic shock of the nasal passages.

Get stuck in rictus position.

Not having that.

No I'm fine.

Everything's fine.

TED. I hate it when you say that.

DOLL. Well that's how I feel so – hold on – you can't just come crawling back – you didn't fucking stand up for me just then. I pissed in a hot tub for you –

TED. Why did you lie, Doll?

DOLL. Because I… I…

TED. But she can't seem to answer me.

So I stand there for a really long time.

Just staring at the little dribbly bit of blood that has poured down her chin, on to her school skirt and will be there forever, knowing Doll and her lack of personal hygiene.

I just stand there staring.

And it looks like – and I just say it:

'Just pretend you lost it.

Just pretend you had a miscarriage – '

DOLL. he says.

TED. Doll locks herself in the loo for the rest of the afternoon – I tell people she's gone home. No one is even listening. I have sixteen Snapchats on my phone and all of them are Doll getting her nose punched in.

As the final bell rings I stand outside the girls' toilets till the whole school is empty – but she's not moving and Doll, well you've figured out by now, she's pretty stubborn.

I stand there till my numb legs take me home on autopilot.

Dad's waiting for me.

My dinner is cold but he's used to that.

I eat the crusts.

He tousles my hair and sighs a little.

Doll – can you do my dad in this bit?

DOLL. No I can't, now hurry up.

TED. 'No wonder you're so small' he says.

'Good things come in small packages.'

Mum's line not his.

And I know that I need to be her friend for real this time.

She didn't mean it to be a lie. Not in that sense of the word, she didn't mean for it to not be the truth. Does that make sense?

I need to come up with a better plan.

I had a plan you see – can you see now, / Doll

DOLL. If everyone wants me not to have this.

If everyone is so certain it's a bad thing.

Then why do people have kids?

Why did Mum and Dad have me if they didn't really love each other?

How old are you supposed to be?

What age do you get good at looking after things?

When you stop leaving your retainer in your Tupperware?

When you clean your own PE kit?

When?

I don't really get it.

I don't get why wanting this is a bad thing.

And maybe I have gone a bit too far.

Why did no one stop me / then?

TED. I did – I / tried

DOLL. I get home from school and Mum comes home to change for the night shift.

You have to do this bit, Ted, I can't physically do it myself you prick…

TED. I just don't think I'm very good at her bits – I mean she's way harder to do than Samantha Hogan.

DOLL. Fine I'll just tell everyone that you wank off to Freddie Mercury.

TED. Doll!

DOLL. 'You're just a poor boy, from a poor family.'

TED. Fine! Fine –

'Gotta wear something lush down the pub, it's our early May Day bank-holiday special.

Chicken korma for two for one – I came up with it – Denny thought burgers but I just thought where's the imagination in that.'

DOLL. Mum?

TED. 'Ha.'

DOLL. Mum.

TED. 'Men.'

DOLL. Mum?

TED. 'What, luv?'

'Feel it kicking can you?'

'Or have your waters broken?'

'Ha.'

DOLL. No...

But –

TED. 'But what, dear, is it time for the little baby Jesus to rear its holy head?'

DOLL. She's a bit drunk – she always is now – the perks of working in a pub I suppose. I always know when she's drunk because her face gets smirky and she gets a bit dribbly at the mouth.

TED. 'You really are an odd one, Doll.'

DOLL. She says.

TED. 'You really are a bit of a fucking freak.'

I'm sure she doesn't call you a freak –

DOLL. Go on...

TED. 'Last time we could handle the lies.'

'We could handle your obsession with Samantha Hogan.'

'God we're lucky they even let you back into the same school.'

'Setting fire to that poor girl's hair.'

You didn't mean to do that, you told me it was an accident –

DOLL. Keep going.

TED. 'Your relentless bullying of that Wong girl.'

Everyone else called her those names too.

DOLL. Ted!

TED. 'The time you told everyone the postman was shagging Shannon's mum which nearly cost her her fucking marriage.'

You made that up? But you –

DOLL. Ted, keep going –

TED. 'Telling everyone such a bunch of lies all the fucking time and now this – '

'And how long – eight months of this I've had.'

'Eight fucking months of indulging this little fantasy – one point I even thought it might be real – hanging out with that boy all the time, I thought okay, okay, if she's really done this we might actually be all right.'

'Then it all just fell apart didn't it, Doll, and I just prayed you'd get tired of it before it was too late.'

'But no you've gone full-out.'

'School ringing me.'

'Asking me if everything's okay at home.'

'I felt like such a shit mum, but it would be worse to be the mum of a nutjob so I told them you were pregnant – that it was all true and the father was a family friend who took it too far.'

'See I can lie too.'

Doll, I don't want to do this bit.

DOLL. Keep going

TED. 'And Denny? He thinks it's true because I'm not going to tell him am I? I'm not going to tell him what a weird, sad family we have – god knows I lost your father I'm not going to lose another, I'm not being humiliated again.'

'Is it attention you want, Doll? Is it? Well guess what, sometimes you have to stop pretending and start being fucking normal for once, life just isn't that exciting, it's a bit shit actually – sometimes you just have to grow the fuck up.'

'How are we going to fix this one, Doll?'

DOLL. She says.

TED. How the hell are we going to fix this?

DOLL. Mum finally looks me in the face then, sees I've got mascara tracks all down my cheeks and all I want is a hug, a cuddle, a duvet full of my mum's arms but instead she goes upstairs, puts a red top on, and leaves.

You gotta solve this one, Doll. Fast.

TED. My various plans include – one: getting Doll pregnant and then just hoping it comes out really early… so a repeat of the incident the other night –

DOLL. We don't ever, actually mention that again actually, Ted.

TED. Right, sorry yeah, um awkward.

Two: stealing a baby and pretending it's hers. Which I'm not sort of okay with morally.

Three: explaining it all as a hysterical pregnancy like in the olden days. You know, Victorian-style.

But none of these will work.

And May 19th is fast approaching.

Bethany's birthday is getting closer by the day.

Which means that Doll's due date is also round the corner.

And I know that, really, the only way out is…

And that's horrid, that's just –

Because in her head it's become real and she just – can't. So I have to do it.

DOLL. Stop pretending you're doing this for me – you're such a fucking liar. You know why you did this. None of this is about me, Ted, it's about her – go on then fucking tell them then – get it off that tiny sad chest of yours. I SAID DO IT.

TED *begins*.

TED. Fine.

My sister was sixteen when it happened, which is how old we are now.

She was tall for her age and really, really fit.

She had eyes that were bolt-stripe blue and eyelashes that looked like adverts.

She loved our cousin Julia more than anything and Julia was eighteen and had tits that I couldn't stop dreaming about which I know isn't quite right, but, trust me I can't stop thinking about most people's tits, so maybe it wasn't too incestuous… maybe.

Julia leant my sister everything, make-up, shoes, the skirt she was wearing and her vodka.

Julia didn't go home with my sister that night and most of the family still won't talk to her because of it. You see she let Bethany go off with these random men, boys, who knows, the CCTV isn't very clear you see – just blurs and she's gone, like that. And there's nothing more but the broken bones they found a week later. There's not even a glimmer of bolt-stripe blue you can see in her eyes and they won't let my mum identify her – upsetting apparently. So I never really got to see what she looked like. But I see her every time I close my eyes.

Mum couldn't live with us any more after it happened, sort of coped and then just sort of flipped it, one day the paper had Bethany's picture on it, all the papers did, and it was one from school, skirt rolled up and her hair down – none of it allowed and she looked like a right slag, my sister, she had her tongue out and her piercing looked like a bit of printing gone wrong. Mum shuddered and remembered fighting with her about that, threatening to 'pull the fucking thing out because it would probably just get infected'. Mum came home with a stack of *Sun*s and *Echo*es and burnt them all in a mess in the garden. Then went upstairs into her room and started dry retching, heaving, shouting 'I can't get it out'. My dad took her paper-black hands and wrapped himself around her, told me to 'get her passport, son, be a good lad'.

She lives with Uncle Stanley who only has one leg – gout ate the other one – in a pub on a port near Marbella and she is beginning to slowly be, not happy, but normal. She sends us postcards of dancers with frilly bits that stick out, they never say very much.

So that's why I was mad at you, Doll, because you had lied to me about the one thing I had left to keep me going, when my family was basically one big shitty mess, had taken away from me the one chance I had of bringing my mum back. You lie all the time, Doll, I know that, but I didn't think you would lie to me.

In my sleep I see my sister climbing over a fence she shouldn't have climbed with the men she shouldn't have trusted and I think about the voicemail she left me – 'cover for me' was all it said and I didn't want her to be blamed any more than she already had been.

Don't you get it, Doll – I didn't want them to do to you, what they did to her.

I'm not letting that happen, the faces and the laughing, Samantha Hogan putting it on Facebook and no one ever, ever, ever forgetting. Her name and number all over the boys' toilets, the way they talk about her – the ones who slept with her acting like it makes them special. The next-door neighbours tutting like they knew it would happen. Like she had it coming. The whole school still posting pictures of Bethany all over my profile like it's nothing. Like I don't see her walking down the stairs every morning. Fucktards the lot of them. Fucking fuck… shit.

What were you thinking, Doll?

DOLL. I didn't know that, about your mum, Ted –

TED. Okay, Ted, plan, and I have the plan, because it had already hit me but I just didn't want to say it out loud, because in a way it makes me a bit sick. But I reason with it, I'm doing this to save her –

DOLL. 'Sometimes, son, you have to make sacrifices in life, that's why we had to let your mother fly away from us, because it was the bigger thing to do.'

TED. Yes, Dad, you were right. Thanks for being my dad, Doll…

DOLL. Just… just get on with it…

TED. And it might mean I never get her back, Mum or Doll,
or Dad. But I can handle it, if only she's spared the brunt
of this.

That's why I did it, can you understand why, / Doll?

DOLL. When Mum leaves I sit there on the sofa, cuddling the
cushion that smells of sicked-up winergy and make a pact
with myself – I know what I have to do – I have to keep this
baby. Because it's real to me. It's a living, breathing thing.

So Ted and everyone else can just fuck off for fuck's sake
and no I do not say hello to Mum in the morning and
certainly not to Denny who keeps pissing with the door open
like he's trying to show off or something. Dick.

I lug myself to school, getting heavier and heavier with my
hood up and my duffel coat choking me, even though it's
really friggin' hot today. Queen Bey screaming *Lemonade* in
my ears, and the feel of something dark and angry inside of
me, want to lash out and hurt someone, probably got to be
Ted really, for abandoning me – thinking should I just punch
his little shitty nose, or really kick him in the testes watch
him gasp to breathe? Pants him in front of the whole class
and laugh at his crappy little y-front baby-boy pants, fucking
cunt bag. Bag of cunts.

I get carried away with all these nasty little thoughts till he's
right there in front of me, looking sheepish like a little
scaredy sheep and I just think, oh, oh no I couldn't hurt him
one little itty bit.

I can't.

TED. I think we almost made up just then – she almost went to
take my hand and everything, but thought better of it. Just.
I can't give in to her, and I don't know if that makes what
I'm about to do better or worse. I start sweating this really
rank onion smell like I'm already guilty.

'Let's…

DOLL. be friends again' he says and he takes my hand and tells
me he's so happy I'm having this baby and he'll get a job as

soon as we finish exams and we'll get a place just us and like raise it together but also have really great boyfriends who share the housework.

TED. 'No, Doll', I say – 'Let's bunk Maths and meet up around the sports block, to like, talk and stuff.'

DOLL *doesn't respond*.

Doll... Doll?

And she agrees.

DOLL *doesn't respond*. TED *carries on regardless, nodding as if she's just agreed*.

And I am relieved – even though I really like Maths and it's the beginning of coursework and actually a really important lesson. But maybe not as important as what's about to happen...

DOLL. Which is that we leave school and tell everyone to go fuck themselves and I open a fashion shop on the high street and everyone thinks I'm like the world's-best-entrepreneur-type thing, and me and my kid are featured on magazines / and

TED. We plan, actually, to meet at the vending machine in the sports block as all the other ones were banned to cut down on fat kids.

That's in three hours' time – end of Maths is start of lunch. Yeah busy time, maximum impact, I can't give her a way out, too easy if no one's around.

Maybe my mum will understand if I can tell her the reasons, in a few years or something.

DOLL. I don't think she will, Ted, and anyway – we end up going to live with your mum in Marbella and we open a club and / we

TED. Three hours pass and I'm at the vending machine and she's got her hand up the mouth bit except her little bump is making it hard to get proper stuck-in.

I help her get a Mars bar and a pack of Soft Mints.

TED *nods to* DOLL. DOLL *won't respond.*

'Result' she says and all is almost forgiven.

I don't say very much but then that's usual.

Isn't it, Doll?

Come on, Doll!

DOLL. I tell him that a few more trips like this and I might be his best mate again.

His smile looks so sad, but then he's always a bit sad that one.

Think he always will be actually.

TED. She makes me smile, when really I want to laugh, but I can't seem to open my mouth. I offer her my Twix, she looks at it for a second, like a girl would, then gobbles it like she would.

DOLL. 'Eating for two ain't I anyway' –

TED. and she stares me out as if to say agree or else…

So I nod, because my jaw still doesn't seem to want to crack a syllable.

Until I force it open with clenched fists and almost shout in her face.

'I don't want to be your mate any more.'

And she says…

And she says…

Come on, Doll…

Say something.

Fine.

Five minutes to get her to the main staircase, I'm going to have to go guerrilla on this one.

I said 'I hate you, Doll.'

Well come on.

DOLL. Maybe we could stop now?

TED. And I grab her backpack and run with it – egging her on, like we're children in the playground, fucking chase me then?!

And inside I'm pleading:

Please follow me.

Please forgive me.

And she's out of breath by the time we reach the back staircase to the second floor. 'Come and fucking get me' I say.

DOLL. Please, Ted, could we –

TED. 'Come and get me then, you fucking freak!'

DOLL. 'I'm going to fuck you up, you fucking ballbag.'

TED. And she clambers up the stairs like it's nothing, bump swinging and it makes me squirm now that I know that there's nothing there but padding, but that's what helps me know she might be okay – make it softer on her – please I pray, don't let this actually hurt her. But I suppose that's the effect I'm going for.

We're at the top, two minutes till the bell goes, pupils pushing back chairs, angry stares, bags already packed, people poised to run for the door on the first ring of that ding...

DOLL. And nothing happens and nothing happens and nothing happens and nothing happens and nothing happens / and nothing happens and

TED. I push her. I push her. I push her.

And she falls

And rolls

And bumps

And her hair swirls

And her eyes are squeezed shut

And her arm pulls out at one point to grab for the rail

But then she's there at the bottom

And the bell just keeps ringing

And she opens her eyes and looks at me and –

There's people everywhere, teachers and Year 7s and one girl's screaming and people are saying 'get the school nurse' like she'll know anything.

And I hate myself for this bit, it's not heroic, but I run down the stairs myself, 'DOLL' I shout 'shit and fuck, someone call her mum'. I get her phone out her bag and do just that – can't let an ambulance get their first.

Only a few people turn to look at me oddly, 'you push her or she fall, man?' and I don't know what to say.

'She's gunna lose that baby that's for sure' says one slightly older kid, a flippant upper-sixth who sucks her teeth at the injustice of it all.

DOLL. My head

Like a spin cycle

Bicycle wheels

Sudden stall

Lifted up by the gym teacher's arms

I feel a bruise pumping on my brainy bits and my elbow bits

And my ankle bones are feeling all lumpy

I shut my eyes again, because the image of Ted's face is all I can see and he looked like a knight all shining but also like he had devil's flames licking round the side of him.

Then I'm in Mum's car and I can tell because of the smell of that fruity fucking perfume and I'm plonked down on the squishier side of the passengers seat, the ripped-up footwell bit. We're racing away and Mum's saying 'don't worry about an ambulance, I can get her there just as fast.'

'I don't think I've broken anything. Mum, I don't think…'

She pulls over in a deserted car park near the Nature Centre that's no longer open or cared for and sits me up, takes off my buckle, takes off my bump. 'Enough of this now. It's done, Doll, thank fuck for that lad he did you a favour, you'll realise that in a bit.'

Will I, Ted? Will I realise that?

She's taking it away from me all bundled up, it's not even ready yet. Not cooked, Mum, not there yet.

And then I'm empty and it hurts, fuck it really hurts and there's a bit of me deep inside that's wailing like a wolf mouth just howling and I tell Mum it's hurting, Mum, I feel something slipping, something dripping. 'You just need some arnica' she sighs, fuck that this is serious I know there's something really wrong about this. I can feel a funny warm thing trying to get out, which in a way feels like it's happening for real, it is real, isn't it? Isn't it?

And I see Mum smile because it's over and everything can 'go back to normal' but my heart is shrinking and I don't think it can ever grow back.

TED. The school halls are stood still.

They all go for the option that I pushed her – it makes sense.

I can feel a fear growing that to be around me is simply unlucky…

And I am relieved by every nasty word that seeps round the school.

I'm sorry, Doll, but I did the right thing.

For you.

I did the right thing.

I'm kept in the nurse's office for the rest of afternoon – none of the teachers say anything, they just tell me to wait but I keep hearing the squeak of people's shoes and the voices of those who know they have to 'do something about it'. They just haven't decided what yet.

My dad bursts in and I go to hug him as usual but he doesn't let me near him. He's looking at me so hard his eyeballs might burst – 'what were you thinking of' he screams at me in a quiet way and I see that all I've really done is made this so much harder for us both. I can't speak, and neither can he.

DOLL. I have a few days off even though the doctor says I'm fine and she even says that sometimes heavy periods can be a sign of stress and I think yeah, yeah I've had plenty of that mate recently, but she still asks if I'm feeling mentally okay because my mum says I've been acting oddly. I've already had professional help, Jesus people don't bother to check do they nowadays, she clearly ain't really bothered. 'Can I go now?'

TED. I'm still suspended pending further action. No charges are bought against me –

Doll's mum is 'keen to put the past behind her', but she won't let me see her, and the sad thing is that it's not even her mum's decision but Doll's.

DOLL. So for days I am holed up all cosy like in bed doing some serious checking of my Facebook profile. Seems they are all sending me love now or something and even Samantha Hogan says we should totes meet up and 'talk about my experience'. When I go round hers all the girls are there and I think it might be an ambush and they are finally going to set fire to me, but they just hug me and make me cry and tell me that they knew it was him, that he was the weird one really.

TED. Another week goes by and I am expelled. Mum comes home. She hates being back in the house, the street, she feels like she's being watched all the time and she jerks her head like a little bird every time someone parks nearby.

DOLL. They sit there and say nasty, nasty worm-like things about him and I let them feed me because apparently I just need some looking after. His locker is empty and no one knows where he is and after a while he has supposedly left the country, well fuck him then.

Fuck you for leaving me.

TED. It is possibly worse than when Bethany died because
    then we had each other but now we can't lift our eyes to
    one another and it gets so bad that one day she just ups
    and leaves again and Dad is so tempted to do the same.
    I don't know why he stays with me – I think he just decided
    a long time ago that I was his responsibility. That he is
    stuck to me.

DOLL. I have other friends now, loads of them, so I don't need
    no psycho like him hanging round me, and the worst thing, is
    that they all think that maybe he had something to do with
    what happened to his sister, well think about it, it makes
    sense dunnit? He likes to hurt people, fucking freak. Likes to
    hurt vulnerable people like her and me. And I'm glad he's
    out of my life – because well he got what he deserved really.
    We both did.

TED. I am not admitted to any other school in the area and
    instead have tutoring for a bit – and then I don't really leave
    the house for a while. Which is sort of actually okay by me.

DOLL. Eventually I leave home and go and live with Dad
    and Auntie Cheryl round the corner, that's when Mum
    finally lets Denny move in properly and my room becomes
    a shrine to all things home-brewery. I do all right in
    sixth-form college, though Samantha Hogan doesn't keep
    in touch like she said she would and I find that all I really do
    is sit in my pyjamas in Auntie Cheryl's spare room and play
    on my iPhone.

TED. When Dad gets transferred to a firm up north you can see
    that he is so relieved – 'But we won't be here for Bethany'
    I say – as if her ashes on the green were enough of a reason
    to stay, it's not even as if anything has grown there since.
    'It's just dead' he says. 'We can't stay round here.' So we
    drive and relocate and eventually I think they get divorced
    but nothing is really said.

DOLL. And I get really really good at Candy Crush Saga until
    Dad says I can only stay if I get a job and I do, and I sit and
    rot for a bit whilst ticking boxes and stealing stationery and
    no one really talks to me.

TED. And we live there in happy silence till I get a job and then my own room in a shared house full of strangers and it's cheap enough and one day I am at a motorway service station driving around on weekends because it's just something I like to do – and I see her.

DOLL. I see him by the fridges that smell of cooling fluid and spilt Ribena and the light is so bright and sterile so we can see each other so very, very clearly really. No hiding here. It has been, what, five years, yeah and I am wearing heels and looking like a right slag because I am driving out of town to meet a nice man I met off the internet and we are having a weekend together, just us – because that's how it is nowadays – and I work hard all week and I like to have these sort of mini-breaks, because that way you don't have to make anything real.

TED. And I wonder if she recognises me, because well I'm a bit taller, just a bit, and I've grown a beard – well stubble and I'm wearing glasses because I finally caved in and stopped pretending I didn't need them. And I think – what do I actually look like, to her – who does she think I am? Because she looks different and the same all at once.

DOLL. For a second I think, what if he was the man I was meeting, and we could just get in the car and drive off together. I watch him and he can't seem to pick anything up because we are both now watching each other move around and around this shop. I could, couldn't I – shouldn't I?

TED. But she doesn't and neither do I.

TED *leaves the stage*. DOLL *is alone*.

DOLL. It was the summer holidays, camping, Wales – not much of a – but you know. So there was Mum on one end of the caravan looking at Dad's honeymoon snaps on Facebook. And there was I just looking at Samantha Hogan's holiday in Ibiza – on her Instagram. Constantly. What a holiday. So it's just me and Mum seething in a tin box on wheels, occasionally leaving to visit monasteries and churches and talk to other angry bitter divorced women on walking tours. And one day

we go into this church and it's raining, really raining – like it
has been all bloody week but all of a sudden, after all this time
– the sun comes out – shines through the windows – you know
the windows with the pictures in them. And they just fucking
light up the whole place, blues and yellows and reds and it's
the Virgin Mary holding her baby boy, and the Virgin Mary
next to her dying boy, and lambs and blood and angels. And
I feel mental. I feel like something has just pulled out my heart
and made me understand everything and nothing. I'm not
saying I found God, because honestly I know Mum is, but I'm
not – but there was something in those pictures, the way they
shone. I wanted to feel purposeful. I wanted to feel like I could
love something better than anyone had loved me. And when
everyone got back after the summer holidays they were all
showing off their tans right, and there was me showing off my
pregnancy test and fainting in class and telling them all about
my holiday romance. Because suddenly we were sixteen and
your only purpose was to have had sex – and I hadn't. I hadn't
come close – but I had changed. I had changed more than any
of them realised. I wanted it to mean something. I still do.

Ted?

Ted?

End.

Other Titles in this Series

'A great published script makes you understand what the play is, at its heart' *Slate Magazine*

Enjoyed this book? Choose from hundreds more classic and contemporary plays from Nick Hern Books, the UK's leading independent theatre publisher.

Our full range is available to browse online now, including:

Award-winning plays from leading contemporary dramatists, including *King Charles III* by Mike Bartlett, *Anne Boleyn* by Howard Brenton, *Jerusalem* by Jez Butterworth, *A Breakfast of Eels* by Robert Holman, *Chimerica* by Lucy Kirkwood, *The Night Alive* by Conor McPherson, *The James Plays* by Rona Munro, *Nell Gwynn* by Jessica Swale, and many more…

Ground-breaking drama from the most exciting up-and-coming playwrights, including Vivienne Franzmann, James Fritz, Ella Hickson, Anna Jordan, Jack Thorne, Phoebe Waller-Bridge, Tom Wells, and many more…

Twentieth-century classics, including *Cloud Nine* by Caryl Churchill, *Death and the Maiden* by Ariel Dorfman, *Pentecost* by David Edgar, *Angels in America* by Tony Kushner, *Long Day's Journey into Night* by Eugene O'Neill, *The Deep Blue Sea* by Terence Rattigan, *Machinal* by Sophie Treadwell, and many more…

Timeless masterpieces from playwrights throughout the ages, including Anton Chekhov, Euripides, Henrik Ibsen, Federico García Lorca, Christopher Marlowe, Molière, William Shakespeare, Richard Brinsley Sheridan, Oscar Wilde, and many more…

Every playscript is a world waiting to be explored. Find yours at **www.nickhernbooks.co.uk** – you'll receive a 20% discount, plus free UK postage & packaging for orders over £30.

'Publishing plays gives permanent form to an evanescent art, and allows many more people to have some kind of experience of a play than could ever see it in the theatre' *Nick Hern, publisher*

www.nickhernbooks.co.uk

A Nick Hern Book

Epic Love and Pop Songs first published in Great Britain as a paperback original in 2016 by Nick Hern Books Limited, The Glasshouse, 49a Goldhawk Road, London W12 8QP, in association with Showroom and Pleasance

Epic Love and Pop Songs copyright © 2016 Phoebe Eclair-Powell

Phoebe Eclair-Powell has asserted her right to be identified as the author of this work

Cover image: © iStockPhoto.com/YuriyS

Designed and typeset by Nick Hern Books, London
Printed and bound in Great Britain by Mimeo Ltd, Huntingdon, Cambridgeshire PE29 6XX

A CIP catalogue record for this book is available from the British Library

ISBN   978 1 84842 597 2

www.nickhernbooks.co.uk

facebook.com/nickhernbooks

twitter.com/nickhernbooks